Perfume & petrol fumes

Richard Price

diehard
Edinburgh

diehard publishers
3 Spittal Street
Edinburgh
EH3 9DY

ISBN 0 946230 625
© Richard Price 1999

A CIP catalogue record for this book is
available from the British Library.

The Publisher acknowledges the financial assistance of the
Scottish Arts Council in the publication of this volume.

Thanks are due to the editors of the following in which poems in
this collection first appeared: *After the Watergaw, Angel Exhaust,
Ape, Lines Review, Manifest, Markings, New Writing Scotland,
NorthWords, Object Permanence, Southfold,* and *Verse.*

An earlier version of *Marks & Sparks* was published by Akros in
1995 (2nd edition, 1996).

A Spelthorne Bird List was premiered at the Troubadour Coffee
House, Earls Court, in January 1998.

The author is especially grateful to Raymond Friel, David
Kinloch, Peter McCarey, and Donny O'Rourke for their
friendship and advice, to Duncan Glen for his publishing faith,
and to the members of 'The Workshop' for their encouragement
over the years.

Contents

Perfume & petrol fumes

Marks & Sparks

Perfume & petrol fumes

Why I'm am expressive abstractionist

Because everyone is

Because America does not yet need me
Because America has not yet Earned My Love

Because I'm fond of the decorative arts
even endpapers

Because I love faces
in general
in particular

Because Hélion Before
is better after After

Because nobody is

Because I'm also as it were
an Abstract Expressionist

Because dribble's better than drivel
but still dreadfully drab

Because Apollinaire
made the first moon landing

Because beach buggies
are just dinky

Because

of the Wonderful Wizard of Oz

The houseboat

The Thames froze over
and Heather Iona Macgregor Colquhoun
said to me,
        "Shall we
take the kids skating?
While they're practising balance
and learning their gases, liquids and solids
we could have a gander
at that old houseboat, *The Shug MacD*.

You know its bankside windows
are crammed with pamphlets and cracked papers,
with encyclopaedias that regard
the dodo's future
with a degree of uncertainty –
I'd like to walk, glove in glove with you, Murdoch,
to its portholes next to the river
and see, once and for all,
the size of that barge's kitchen.
What do you think?"

Looking up, finally, from the Business and Media Supplement
of my *Scotland on Sunday*,
pausing, it must be said, for some retrospective listening
to retrieve, I hoped, everything
since the sentence I've subsequently learned
was almost definitely
"Shall we bake the squid shaking?",
the word "kitchen" struck me.
It had, I gathered,
been used in a marine context
and surely, therefore, quite inappropriately.

After seven years of a happy Presbyterian marriage, however,
I knew better than to bark
at Heather Iona Macgregor Colquhoun,
especially on such matter as nautical jargon.
Her great-uncle, after all,
had been unemployed in the shipyards.

Instead, folding the portrait of the chief executive
                    of Scottish Television
neatly in half,
so, I recall, that only his smile and his admirable teeth
                    were in view,
I said softly to my wife,
with the gentleness of a man used to, but far from tired of,
the pleasure of intellectual debate with his chosen partner in life,

"Galley, you mean?
Is a boat's kitchen not a galley?"

My wife, sensing (as you know, with good reason),
diversionary tactics,
smiled the briefest of smiles,
looked me – a little too directly – in the eye
and replied:

"Murdoch,
did the University of St Andrews grant you a doctorate
in Scottish Men's Studies
for the benefit of correcting
the vocabulary of a Macgregor Colquhoun?
Was your platter last dinner,
MacSween's Vegetarian Haggis,
developed under meatfree laboratory conditions,
tested first on amoebae, consenting mice, and then, and only then,
on the cream of Scotland's scientific profession,

all for the fuelling of such misconceived pedantry?
Was – ?"

                    and so on,
with fifty-one questions,
until, answering each and all herself
with the sole small word, "No",
'I', as I call her, pointed it out to me
that though, against her better judgment,
she had of course considered the word "galley"
at the end of the day,
weighing one thing with another,
listening to both sides, taking everything on board,
she had been persuaded, compelled, forced,
to rule firmly against.

The craft at issue, she reminded me,
was a *house* boat,
a structure defined primarily
by its domestic function.
She accepted that some may be tempted
in considering this perhaps most anomalous of dwellings
to deem either word equally fitting,
while still others, in the spirit of well-meaning peacemaking,
might designate it "the cook's room", "the bacon booth",
poetically even, "the greedy gimbals",
she (making reference, as predicted,
to her illustrious industrial pedigree)
knew enough about boats, and what went on inside them,
and, for that matter, houses and managing a home,
to rule everything but "kitchen"
absolutely out.

I made no response.

The question, in short, was resolved,
to our joint if not wholly equal satisfaction
(I would like to have enquired
whether "windows" and "portholes", by her own logic,
were quite as interchangeable as her initial speech seemed to imply)
but, recovering the initiative,
I went straight instead
to our shared woollens drawer in the bedroom
and, holding up two pairs of extra-thick socks,
cried, "Tartan,
or plain?"

The Presenter
after Ruaraidh Mac Thomais

That night
a presenter came into the living-room –
a suspiciously ordinary man
in a good suit.
He sat on the couch
and our books
dropped off their shelves
(my wife was in an armchair
humming no. 12 in the charts –
he made *her* feel small).

But he did not leave us empty-handed:
he gave us a new tune,
and tales from the Middle East
and shrapnel from the-philosophy-of-the-Whitehouse,
and he switched the telly on again
and set a gameshow in our hearts.

Truce —

Either
      'bridge between conquerors'
or
      'city of sweet oranges'—

                        a honeymoon.
Certainly, a misnomer
for this most serene
of little capitals,
many kilometres
from 'the basket
of the nation'.
            Personally, I'm against
long lines and the difficult in poems.

                        Difficult
to know what to think —
        about agreement, generosity —
I'm for these.

            But there was something –
                about the tide out –
            just a river – the three bridges –
            grey, all of it, greys
                individuated, all tones
            and the holed boxy boats rested
                on the sludge,
            the islands analogues for holidays
                joined by the mud –

ach, nearly a rhyme —

            but themselves most of all.
And you,

the you.

You there.

A bit more consideration
after Vallejo

Who's making all that bloody noise, and won't entertain
the chance that the rising islands will testify.

A bit more consideration
as it's going to be getting on shortly
and you'd better weigh up
the shite, the simple treasure-ish cadaver-bowf
bestowed, despite itself,
on the insular heart
by the briny gannet, with each transparent squall.

A bit more consideration
and the skitters, six at night
 OF THE MOST MAGNIFICENT BUM-NOTES

And the peninsula rises up
behind, gagged, fearless
on the mortal line of balance.

How's that old country go again?

If the archipelago
was splinters of bone
set wrong, no mending,
the mainland stretched you,
shape-to-shaping, an arm or a cough,
a mini-kilt lilting, hiding, some bright spark
launching his Queen Elizabeth, throwing a Wendy
a semi-detached semi-conductor, yes yes maybe no,
tactful now, the board are listening, [civilization]'s clootie-pudding
(cry it dessert), tweetsweet, sucker, the wedge of a swedger, the thin end.

Mud for the chin

"What's a computer?"
"Eat yourself fitter." – Mark E. Smith

Work at my eyes, vague ball-ache
and a lung-y cough. Hungerford Bridge
here I come.
                              Mum was right
about hair (the cow's lick), skin,
and bad breath. It's mud for the chin, silt.

Talk me out it. Speak softly
from your mockit blanket. Any more help
than "Any spare change?"
                                    Or you two,
office-pinned through your blouse,
by your tie: what's the copier say

my stars have in store? All tomorrow
in the fax's teeth? Control-Alt-Delete?
Sorry. Sorry. Sorry.

Alongside

You're to be admired,
talk to you for
(self to yourself?)
but measured, clear.

Home to keep another
out of a home.
Work to keep another
out of work.

To be referred to,
expertise of my colleague,
help desk
also well-groomed.

Home to keep another
out of a home.
Work to keep another
out of work.

Who you could explain,
up to,
compare, as –
reflect, admire.

Home to keep another.
Work to

The thing is

Drinks on the sills,
folk just their clothes,
and all Covent garden
confidential in public.

Just today, stroke tonight,
don't answer me this:
what was kingship
in Charlemagne's Europe?
Are Germans in tens
to hunt boar in Glen Affric?
Will Mr Alexander
nostril your scent
like a scarf on my coat
on my coat-stand?

This last summer evening,
I think I mean first autumn,
it must be everyone
is beyond their office
(that's just like Gary
when it comes to the follow-up
and you can't blame Systems).

The polls say
we all live in Southampton.
Excepting present company,
you and a cooling million,
I almost –

His mouth, his thumb, his finger

That close up, the thumbprint isn't
a tea-hill.
Back some, no terracing.
Plum
at the end of ability.

Delicate contours.
A trigger crook
I don't think.
Ordnance Survey?
Ballad-land appliqué,
no.

As I walked out I did.

A touch of thumbnail,
thumbnail on tooth.
Forefinger,
bold top lip.

Are you doing anything
TONIGHT?

Horseshoe crab in flagrante delicto

Full moon and a grey piece of the moon
slips out of the restlessness, the sea.
Say a million years, say four hundred,
and begin with her again:
life is lisping in the water,
the Earth is just rising.

As usual, she's lugging her man,
gaining the globby sand.

She'll let him do what she likes,
bury it, and get back.

An abstract spider,
she'll re-enter the fusses of the foam,
see the glint in the deep
and head for that struggling moon,
the moon in the ocean's web,
the moon's mime and its warning.

Lick and stick

"For those who wish to experiment before committing themselves
to an indelible design, there is the temporary tattoo. This uses the
'lick-and-stick' method." *Staple's World of Body Art Website*

It's a pleasure, this
  lick-and-stick of something extinct, flexing,
                the dinosaur you back-classify a dragon,
                    a far, long cry
from the patch on your wrist,
bubblegum scented, a pirate, in orange and green,
a memory before you were ten
but you're fragrant now
as the print is moistened, firmed, as it's pressed
  on the tension of your shoulder,
                smoothed for runkles,
                    and now the graft unpeels
                        skin from skin,
                                no tearing this time,
                                no distortion, this time,
                        this
                            time
'only the mouth
  means more than the skin' –
as you say, you can't talk
                in isolation,
in the shell of your skull
                the tongue's the sealife,
is more than surviving,
                                a little bright tongue
but your lips seem tender
        – expecting a cold?
(this morning, I cut myself shaving,
feel your top lip, swollen)

so today no outré garish tawdry lippie
(the purple so dark it was all but black
in that fancydress bash in Islington –
through your gown your breasts like neat and
                              secret combinations,
                              the door
                                   of your four-square safe,
stroke sea-anemones, suggesting question mark
                         a divable cave?,
got up in screens, an isotope technician, facemask and mitts,
and me, in much the same kit, a halfhearted impression
                         of a cardiac surgeon,
                                        a right pair
)
like the brackets your lips indent on your coverless pillow,
('the mouth,' I lisped, 'is half a kissh')
our parenthesis
                    chit chat
with your theories of flirting and especially skin
containing and hinting,
                         the article of clothing
                              the definite article
more than a wraparound, life-time, one-off sentence –
you can't get away
                    with calling it clingfilm,
you can't dismiss selfgeneration –
delicate skirts (the leather veining
and veiling – re-vealing),
                         the point of gloves,
the emphasis of – switch – your lime pastiche of a cocktail dress,
your lipgloss, of fragrance, so often itself
from specialisation, pungent sophistication, just beneath the flesh,
I mean identifier glands and their pheromones,
'furrymoans', speak in my defence, speaking liquid sugar,
and you own up publically

to threadworms descending, each night entwining
(remember that rave near Wraysbury?)
in the wee hairs of your arse, nibbling
at the dilatable membrane,
picked up, you'll be saying, fifty years on,
'from a squat, pun intended' – in Haringey
or a deb's comingout in Knightsbridge,
but the itch, you say, as if confidentially –
with mock nostalgia – was also an ache,
a yearning, a longing, like the sex of a purse still to be paid for,
your little mocassin with Fort Apache insignia,
and your telling admission, for a lover of serpents and markings,
that you were raised between Slough
  and (your snobbish embarrassment)

                          A Town Called Staines –
proclaimed you say by the Thames, the tattoo of the Thames,
a trumpet solo one side your spine, flowing the length
of your too-often tense back,
the Thames with the head of a snake,
optimistic and exotic, brilliant blue,

                       'woad' you pipe up,
with all the royal houses and the palaces
of riverside stations, slipways and wharfs,
their names and your birthdate, your epitaph (ominous space underlined)
                       in calligraphy,
                in words with edges,
and the river's free verse I have to insist
relying on pattern and the shape that contains it,
its flexible volume, its brimming, er-hm, genius
for composition (like the peach-, conch-like birthmark
                the other side your vertebraes,
                   facing
  the tidal reaches),
its genius for composition, for perspective and rubbish
like the breath that's got snagged

between m'mouth and ma lungs
as I wait on your lips, on your larynx, on your tongue,
the proof of telepathy, the uh-huh or nuht,

                                        the pleasure
of more than that show you swear you curated
of broch stones and bells from the first Chinese dynasty
and prostitutes' callcards from phonebooths in Bloomsbury,
Little Miss Delhi, "Goa", Night Nurse and Rose,
with the kitsch of correction, of distraction, of
                                        girls in their teens,
knickers from hospitals with x-rated xeroxes
of backsides and aprons –
an exhibition – an obsession –

                                with husks and small traces,
with scrapings and leavings, like the scratches in Orkney
of Vikings on holiday on the island prehistory urgently claims,
in that old cemetery, 'in this infirmary',
in postmodern games of quote
                                touching all but fertility,
leaving filaments to tease between juices,
                                        to stretch
like rubber
   tapped from forests of delivering other" –
                        Christ, your Catholicism
rubs off quickly,
                   kicks in, I should say,
as unguents crack
                   the whip of the synapse,
and you've gone and come back
                        (shoulders, more carefully uncovered)
and won't be put down
as a leaver or lover, as no-ing or yes-ing,
of deciding a future, a rhythm or structure –
'You yourself aren't above it, beneath more like,
and no moral amoral artist scruples –

18

you'll be muttering freedom before you're quite finished –
something to do
                        with as close as possible
and still not knowing up to the minute, the whole shebang,
                                    the aphtha and swarfega,
with tasting just a layer, where underwear were, whatever wherever –'
like the perfume you'd expect a younger woman to wear
or barely scent, just the ghosts of shampoo
                                squirt-measured this morning,
hair in the sink, darker for water,
but you're your father's daughter, adopted, just want to talk
                        critiques of dirt, of giving, of the body as art,
of what's gritty, what's earthy.
what's squalid, what's evil,
what's bitter, what's *what*,
(Doc Dwarf to Snow White –
'What are you,
                and who are you doing?')
'what's it all worth' –
                        as I lie here beside you
in my skin and my name, in my dreams
(the ink is smudging,
no joke, the dragon's just smoke),
Rory Sangster v Terry Lean,
I mean
   who are you?, which much?
                I've always hardly known you,
will you
        be in touch?

19

Auto-teller

Beyond a cashpoint
court shoes rub concrete
(your quilted jacket, you in it).
You're jigging to keep warm.
Not a nursery rhyme,
you look sixteen and the benefit.
It's late.
The strap of your bag
crosses your heart.

Light dreeps from this double-decker,
it falls through the eye
of a peacock feather, a puddle,
gets up bruised.
Now it's smudging something
shiny you're wearing,
patting the corrugations
of your deep red corduroy skirt.

Your face, your red hands.

The bus clears its throat.
I can't see you now.

Lifers

Out of you, out of me, a glob rests on your hard-pressed hairs,
a menhir of gel on pubic slaves (us laughing it off, laughing
it on, tremendousing a duvet around us, lifers, under blankets,
yet to be sentenced).

Club mix

The rushes good, as good, and drum 'n' bass,
the, that's the soundtrack, bass, and melody
set back and pretty, from a, think she danced,
before you came the night you couldn't, say
she did then, T-shirts, mauve-white, U.V., all
a rush to head, that's blood I mean, how d'you,
the risk, the bends, the tightened drums, and bass
the tracks of sound, the stripes, the grid of light,
the drum, the drum. The bass, the drum. The drum.

Out take

His talking voice – asking for help. Wire the mike
to this heart, more of the man, stick that
that's a guitar and shriek then, squealer,

take this I'll-not-take-it and wail,
scowl, shout,

still not enough, loser,
still –

Ach, leave it.

> *You want tae leave it?*

Leave it, Toni.

> *You want tae leave it?*

> *What happened?*
> *Take it from take this?*

Out take and receiver

Scowl, but
that's not the shape of a limo's back window,
every hotel's hydroponics, courtesy soaps, matt black
of amp and swing-snecked equipment packs –
the children phoning from 'home'.

'Darlin, put your Ma on the line.'

Out take and transformer

The keyboard's delicately through you,
the dry twitch of the drum's cut stripes on your arms,
blood slashes, carcass-man, Sergeant Rib,
that's your voice then, no howl, no squawk now,
just you, telling yourself through your teeth,
pay for it

redeem

(who'd forgive you?).

Tribute to a mouth

I hang the flatfish of the socket guitar
by the smile of its palette. This is to say
the blues must.

The trumpet that made you has wept and sweated.
You broke the pistons and the corners of mouths.
This is to say the blues must

(reach their confinement).

Between us

Entre nous,
Europe made me money tonight.

Just between us, right,
Scotland made me money tonight.

Between you and me, hen,
gender made me money tonight.

Between you and me, me and you,
Bakhtin made me money tonight.

"Between" 'us', squiggle,
$L = A = N = G = U = A = G = E$ made me money tonight.

Betweenthefuckinperruvus,
swearie words made me money tonight.

Between us.

A Tapestry

Here is Eve.

This was the Tree, and this the Serpent
And this was the Mynah Bird.
The Mynah was still, the Mynah was silent,
And this was the Tale he heard:

'The Fruit is rich, the Fruit is sweet.
The Fruit will cure your Thirst.'

'I'm not sure. It isn't right.
Can't you try first?'

That was the Story – quite sufficient
For the Mynah in the Tree.
He clicked his Beak above the Serpent
And flew his Tale to Me.

I am Adam.

Tilt

The loved
fine-tune their pillows,
adjusting to absence, low-voiced radio.

Across underpasses a car herds light.
Junction gantries
tilt a man between women.

A station fuzzes.
Eyes keep the road.
Fingers feel the waveband

into the clear.

Larkfinchfish! Larkfinchfish!
Lark! Finch! Fish!

Above the cursus a lark tunes a radio:
no stations, intricate interference.
We are balancing in the field
or not hearing trumpets
when trumpetfinches sing.

The birds boom in the glued oasis.
Jeeps and a junior synthesiser
re-describe them:
wheelspin bird,
Bontempi linnet.

Or we're swimming an eyed gulf:
a Picasso triggerfish –
a Kalashnikov in a blue period
(Guernica on a machine-gun's butt) –
gasps within its name.

Larkfinchfish! Larkfinchfish!

Lark!

Finch!

Fish!

At least two pairs of shoes

A week after new shoes
I've to take the rubbish out
so I slip the old treads on –
they fit lightly,
they understand my feet.

The top of the swing-bin
unbalances in my hands,
I'm easing up
the bag's strained film,
conscious of tomatoes,
tea and old tissues,
gathering two corners
and only just managing a knot.

Outside, the rubbish brings up
rats and teenagers:
both seen recently
being sociable at the bin shelter.
None tonight, of either,
so I hold my breath
among the spills and scraps,
sling the black bag
up into the drum
and head home –
twenty yards to the close.

Back in the house
I slip off my shoes
without solving the laces,
stand them by the new.
I know the replacements
are as clumsy as clogs

28

but their leather
is so aromatic –
they are smooth to see,
to touch, and
they are pure pure black.

They are shoes
I will not
be seen dead in.

A private road

The private road the compact special ambulance
decelerates into, gets used to, power steers
across and round, can bear a car that's not a hearse
yet not for life. The undertaker's gates unearth
and level grey unmetalled dirt. The road's resettled, firmed.
Long tinny family cars with seatbelts caught in doors
play jeep on top of pressed remains of rucks and dips,
and opposite the maisonettes and garage row
the sawnoff tubing that's a train in dressage mode
assiduously canters on its shoved-up slope.
The cherry tree that froths beyond the lacy fence
beneath the tracks, is thanks, the mums insist, to spit.

Ad

An advert for a network owned by all –
'a network' – trains and buses, water, fuel,
and information, housing, health as well,
and most of all a sense of life, of small
accomplishments achieved within a frame –
and busy! – matted with invention, bright
and hopeful, knowing it's a hope – a time
to direct (as it's never quite too late) –
it's that I see tonight. I have to speak,
phone in to those who'll hear, and those who won't.
You have to say it once. It's for the sake
of possibility you don't recant.
Just thirty seconds – zero time to lose –
to film the future, storyboard the news.

Sleeplessness for the rest

Don't smile, miracle manager from boss school,
I'm not pally with folk who lead by flipchart,
who can't add or own up to ('Simply No Choice') –
who blame juniors at annual reckoning time.
I know, after your management consultants
brief you (Re the Redundancies), you can leave, too:
the dream job is awaiting Mr Planned Growth.
Sleeplessness for the rest – 'that *is* a downside' –
so you're grave, confidential-like, allow doubts
their margins. 'The, the risks I've taken, real risks.'

1. How can a society survive you?

Tights

Tights are dark in their packet. It is difficult to judge the precise shade they will be. The colour in the small window is the colour of a concentrate – for life, just add legs.

Tights out of their parcel begin in the hands as dense manacles but as they are carefully unrolled it seems as if these ankle-shackles will dissolve into nothing. They become thinner and thinner as they are unfurled higher and higher over their owner's shaven calves and thighs. Finally, they enclose almost half the body.

They are sometimes said to be man-traps, but when women go out in them it is women they keep in. They may tear, but they will not break: they can repair broken-down cars.

They are 'man-made', meaning they are made by machines operated largely by women and children. Through mass production they offer 'free market democracy'. A product of the West, they darken white skin, a compromise imposed on Africa.

Tights are a work of art. The delicacy of their tone is not to be matched in the most accomplished studies of light and shade, since life moves them, and they are part of that life.

As they disappear up beneath a skirt's hem, they continue a classical tradition.

They are the closest clothes can be to being nothing without being nothing. They are the nearest fabric to perfume.

Agitprop
After Mayakovsky

Agitprop – I feel it
like a sicksworth of medicine
slooshing
between tonsils and teeth.

I'd love to jot down
a few lovely love songs
for you and your lovely lot –
with a gemutlich Mittel Europ tune –
with the right producers –
I'd be sure to land cash.

Agitprop!
I can hardly
contain myself.

Deportment

A plane with a bump on its head
lowers its clutch of wheels
and the test is over
for the hypothermic stowaway.

He turns up, early for work,
an impact on the car park
of Commercial Voice and Data.

His brother
survives the amateur cryogenics,
an IOU for A & E,
refugee remand.

Just one last trip
on the world's favourite airline
then –

securely home.

Academic related

Reading the Vacancies Supplement
the VSO is talking Sahel
or singing Verb-Subject-Object.

Basque is not a teddy.

I said language, narrative, closure,
dialogic and deconstruction
(I think you said postmodern
for the same reason).
They used to say dialectic,
class struggle,
and now I've caught myself
with 'hegemonic',

like waxed appleskin
between my teeth.

Till the day I come back
After Vallejo

Till the day I come back, from this chuckie
my heel of authority
will be born, its crime spree, its ivy,
its actor's stubbornness, its olive tree.

Till the day I come back, in pursuit,
as decent – as candid – as the bitter disabled,
wandering, well to well, I'll find out
what's got to be good is people.

Till the day I come back and till the
animal me walks between his judges,
our brave pinkie will be mighty,
dignified, an infinite finger among digits.

Promise?

A promise, this, a path between two reservoirs
that holds those liquid plateaux back, that yields
to not a menace nor a gash in flood –
no guided bombardment – that's just a line
between pre-tensioned brackets (back to front
and paragraphs attached, clauses to scrap),
a phrase to outlive first and final draft,
accomplished from its infancy and still
articulate at ninety, quickly made
like all humanity compared to time,
yet timeless now, this settlement, this vow.

Speaking up

Painted spoken.
Printed ... here.

Time,
as it were.

For reference,
having to refer.

To speak out,
speaking up for.

Saying, say.
Sayings from over there.

Hearings.
Hearing her.

Shh.

Star.

Marks & Sparks

Fishbones of aerials

An aerial: on a stick,
straight skeletons of fish.
A wok for the satellite dish,
nothing cooking.

A week past and counting
we tutted at the news, whatever,
eat together the hit-or-miss:

I talked myself to this,
out the recipe, the safe side
of the ledge.

I hear, like an empty fridge,
half rattle, half hum,
Eat the telecoms.

Kids

The window's open, the tree are fresh.
The kids know happiness
and they're kicking it between them.
I hope they hit our door.

I'd ask you for a game
but I've been told before.

Wasps

Autumn's here, the wasps
are trying to get in.

Home
is my crime too,
hope the sin.

Last Spring you broke in,
took ... everything.

Separate again

Come back to bed, forget the money.
When I said you needn't worry
I was thinking, 'separate again'.
Hear my sorry. Tell me when.

"Leave your keys by the mat:
we'll pick things up
after that."

Wrong again

The taste of you
is strong on my tongue.
Let me go – I won't be long.
I'll get dressed and write the song
that tells our friends they were wrong.

You are
here for good?

Careless

I care for you.
You ... could care less.

You cannot persuade
tenderness.

That's after hurt,
half-forgetting harm,

thinking you could know
a careless man.

Behind you

I love you.

I'm nostalgic
for us and this table,
note the cups piled up.

I said nothing at work.

That painting behind you
is yours, a gift,
figurative and sensual
(open, even so, to abstraction).

The clock can't be read
on Assurance Buildings.

Remember instead
(rain tomorrow, too)
you were you, we were us,
I was mine.

It was
British Summer Time.

Helpline

It's your life,
but I don't trust you with it.
You hark back to "us".
I've lost track of it:
if that was love
you shouldn't ... trade on it.

You've not been charged
for this call.

Marks and sparks

Of course I'm a novice,
meaning you're not?
I don't think so.

If it's not Marks and Spencer's,
product-tested,
what you're got up in
and how you're getting out it
still speaks volumes
(mail order,
or is it TV shopping?).

As you're anxious but asking
to open your shivering legs
I'll own up –
I'm out of myself
with nervous excitement,
hope I don't
cough cough,
flood the two-stroke,

and I suppose your husband
fits like the proverbial
(my ex used to ...).

Can I hurry you?

Deli

You're transparent – heart
in a twist of clingfilm,
lungs, flap flap flap.

Still fresh, those
other organs?
Talk about that?

(Behind the counter
your daughter's mother
offers you up.)

Twigs

Twigs mark my back in the Manor's wood,
twigs mark yours when we turn.
Taste of your mouth
and the smell of the wood,
heat of sweat returned.

Say you forget it now,
say you don't quite recall.
I know you're living it again,
I know you're seeing it all.

You're here with me in the Manor's wood,
you're here now – just like then.
"Over," you say,
"It's over for good.
Nothing happens again."

Less said

Though you left me
I worry about you.
Are you with someone
unsuitable?

The last time,
etcetera.

Sleep again, 'sleep' –
saying more then
than between
Kilmaurs and Kilbarchan,
the going good.
I was ...

not as good as this.

Start again?
Find someone ...

unsuitable?

I wish

"Let me down
at the bus bay?"

Hazard lights, idling,
wipers' tongues

dry, off. "I,
I wish you well."
"I wish *you* well."

Actually holding hands.
"Friends?"

"You'll miss your."
"I'll miss my."

"I wish...
I wish."

Passenger side

You flourish, alone.
For a second
even this face

could be a memory,
as yours is,
is so.

We both look back –
the car's the sound
of its own reversing,

suffered that quick
on the one way.
"The post box is fine.

Promise you'll read?"

Shoosh

Because
you were just like her,
she wasn't you.

Six years later, Sheila,
I remember your "Shh,"
our bodies
a greedy mouthful
on the hungry bed.

Today, your double's
unfashionable,
she wears your coat,
your conservative shoes ...

When she looks,
"Shh," I say to myself
without beginning your name.

'Skirt'

Feet more delicate than yours
slant out from the duvet.
On the carpet a skirt
catches its breath;
that scent you avoid
pretends it's *deja vu*.

My hands, I trust,
are not someone else's.

Fitted sheet

Now that we've untidied ourselves
kneel with me in our laps.
A kiss for our clothes' volcano –
that damp ash –
a kiss for that bing of slack.

On the puckered fitted sheet,
one alert, one asleep.

Engagement / Strike

After I happened
to know your label,
you container
for thing contained

we belonged
to our own bodies,
strikers maybe,

had, anyway,
to repeat ourselves,
a banner for our bed.

What that
explicit slogan said
is unreadable,
unread.

On, off, over

I love you,
and you,
and you

now sleeping, top on
from slipped off, finally,
over your shoulders,

now sleeping, not one
thought for me,
rightly,

now sleeping, right,
not a thought.
You were wrong.

I love you.

Think for thinking

When will we be ...
gentle again?

An eye-headache, car-noise.
We're wearing our foreheads,
offering ... short tempers.

We're lessening

but the money and the space
and the money and the space

keep
on
promising.

Tensioned frame

"Never," by the pylon's feet
a mile from the village sign:
"Never," you said,
and "Only," and "Love,"

                    and "Mine."

"Quiet," in the electric field
beneath the tensioned frame.
"Quiet," I said,
and "Lonely," and "Love,"

                    and "Time."

A new establishment

A sudden weekend.

A friend fresh out of marriage
electrifies our entry-phone;
a backing-singer
pushed to a solo mike.

In our mucky hall
our parents' children's books
buzz like two-stroke engines.
One of us talks down.

When the storm door waives
man-made soles
flap breathily up the steps ...

Later, our visitor in the close again,
the bracelet, the doorchain, is fast.
I unsaddle separates
from the bandy clothes-horse.

On the stereo
a single's black coffee
twirls its central cream.
Like a love-letter

we fold the bed-cover.

Art lover

"Shh, you'll wake the baby," –
first words
when you touch my fists,
tense in the dream.
No, I'm me.

Talk about romance
and you're just talking,
but your kiss,
your lips –

(Either way, I'm not bothered:
if we rise above ourselves
by being what we know we are
or by just denying it) –

you draw your hand
gently down my back,
a confident art-lover,
and you can have me
at almost your lowest bid.

Call

I'm in love with you again
(privilege of elegy, binary of lyric)
and the mynahbird's unlearnt
the car alarm, moved back up
to blackbird, means it love.

You're the nightingale,
singing nightingale
(what's a nightingale
sing like?),

you're –
as if all this time sings up,
our time, our time again,
you, and I must admit,
me,

answering back

As if

All your worries –
forget the lot
and hug me.

Hold's the word,
as if all's been said,
not yet done.

No don't listen to me
religiously.
Just

know I'm yours –
if it's talk, if love.
If love, love.

As, as

What falls between us
is the rain
as thick as, as fast as,

and you're there with your ornaments
and we're here with our tucked-up nets
(say the car-park dividing us joins us),

and the snow
is just heavier than leaves,
just more liquid,
plural as millions et cetera –
it's as fluid I mean
as creamy falling stars

and what falls between us
falls and finishes the.

"Bye," I say, say,
and all of us, well, wave.

A Spelthorne Bird List

The name Spelthorne is a Saxon word meaning
'Speech Thorn Tree'

– John Mills, *A Guide to the Industrial History of Spelthorne*

Hedge Sparrows

You don't see many hedges these days, and the hedges you do see they're not that thorny, it's a shame, and when I say a hedge I'm not talking about a row of twigs between two lines of rusty barbed wire, or more likely just a big prairie where there were whole cities of hedges not fifty years ago, a big desert more like, and I mean thick hedges, with trees nearby for a bit of shade and a field not a road not too far off so you can nip out for an insect or two when you or the youngsters feel like a snack, a whole hedgerow system, as it says in the book, and seven out of ten sparrows say the same, and that's an underestimate, we want a place you can feel safe in again, we're social animals, we want our social life back, and the sooner the better, because in a good hedge you can always talk things over, make decisions, have a laugh if you want to, sing, even with a voice like mine!

Coot

The coot was a pint of stout. It slipped out from The Ferry during a fight. Mathematically white, it was plunged by its beak in mathematical black. To uppity swans it does not signify. The same goes for Joe Duck.

Mandarin Duck

The box of a frozen-food tiramisu misfolded into a crumple. Looking for its reading glasses. Feral in Surrey.

Great Crested Grebe

My favourite bird is the Great Crested Grebe. It's great! The Romans called it *Podiceps Cristastus*. It was almost extinct when Queen Victoria was the Queen, but Aldous Huxley, writer of *Animal Farm*, raised a stink about women's hats. Feathers went out. I think the crest looks like a carpenter's pencil behind the ear, and they do build a nest like an ark. They are brilliant underwater swimmers. My gran says it's a wonder they don't catch polio.

Cormorants

They did not pass the test. Just past the school for private girls, in coats of strips of black blazers, they colonise the flooded pits.

Mallards

A delicate dad caught dabbling in Debbie Duck's drawer – a green glossy popsock caught at head and neck, lycra in chestnut for his chest, grey the rest. In the brown uniform of a money warden his chosen takes five ducklings through their mocks.

Heron

A greying Senior Lecturer in Fish Studies (Thames Valley), he stands in frozen hop concentration, regarding a lectern only he can see. Still, he gets results. He's hoping for a chair.

Swans

Pure snow: the remains of icebergs hauled from the Arctic Circle to cure a drought. Their beaks are municipal clamps.

Swan

A spotless aristocratic glove puppet. Its last song? Opera.

Cuckoo

It's an uplifting call and when you hear it Spring is coming, sure enough, resurrection, promise kept. But I'm not comfortable. That's no life for her and it's no life for anyone else mixed up in the whole business. The parents think the chick is just like them, and it's a hero when it gets bigger. Then it's all me me me, eating its brothers out of home and house, breaking its fostermother's heart as sure as. I can't speak to her about it, and she won't get help. She says: every one of my children is like a little Jesus, and that makes me God.

Pigeons

Pedestrianise the High Street? Crumbs!

Song thrush

Its shirt in ill-advised off-white, customised with blotches of crank-oil, a thrush prods the temporary car park. He/she almost forgets to repeat itself, but on a scaffold a song finds it and finds it again.

Ring necked parakeet

They call us Asians. I deny
nothing, neither grandad nor now.
It's just a collar. Please rely
on other data – know the how
beyond the costume green, the why
escaping when we sing our 'row',
the who our chokers signify:
a chain from chains, as times allow.

Carrion crow

Headquarters could spare only a couple of officers, rheumatics in all-weather macs. But the old boys knew what was what, they knew what wasn't. Measuring the second field, not three metres from the wood's muddy edge, they found the two of them. Four days, maybe five. 'A pact'.

Jay

We packed some snacks, cokes and beer, took the train out to Windsor and walked up to the Great Park. It was September, but as you looked up the avenue there was a heat haze at the knees of the Giant Copper Horse and Horseman. They looked like they were stepping out of the waves, turning, about to bear down on you. 'Oaks this old always remind me of root ginger.' We sat in a tree's shade on the tartan blanket he used to have in the car. A stocky brightly coloured bird, chest pink as a perfume counter, flew down from one of the other trees with an acorn in its beak. 'It's a jay,' James said, 'Jay for Jane,' and then he was off, looking at me, laughing. We were both smiling. 'J., the genesis of Joy, a Joint's full lips, first kiss of the spliff, fragrant Jacaranda. Julep, Juju, too. Jay, trumpet-tumbled gentle Jericho, Japanese pyjamas, ma Jolie Jeune fille, ma Joie de vivre, ma Je ne sais quoi.' 'J.,' he said, with an exaggerated sigh, 'my Jeopardy.' The bird had vanished by the time he was finished that lot. He'd been doing actions. Later on, on the way back into town, I saw another one, quite a way off, though he missed it.

Domestic geese

More woofers than tweeters, they guard Stereo Component with surroundsound.

Moorhen

They push and they push, and it seems to me they never reach the end of their beak – a stop button. And it's like they're made of delicate ashes themselves. Their first flight. Just to commemorate my two and think of them when I come out here.

Magpie

There are winners and there are losers in this life. You might as well be a winner. Motorway verges, council grounds, anything landscaped, fine. Have a recce, see what suits, move in. Some creature gives you a look, take its eyes out.

Kingfisher

Blue. I mean green. Blue, green.   Gone.